MOTTETTI

Poems of Love

1 9 9 0

THE MOTETS

O F

Eugenio Montale

TRANSLATED &

WITH AN INTRODUCTION BY

DANA GIOIA

MOTTETTI

Poems of Love

GRAYWOLF PRESS

SAINT PAUL

1990

These translations have appeared, sometimes in earlier versions, in
Boulevard, Field, Sequoia, and *Translation.* A different version of the
introduction was published in *Boulevard.* The translator is grateful to
the editors of those journals as well as to John Felstiner, who
encouraged me to begin the translations, and Thomas DePietro,
who helped improve the introduction.

Jonathan Galassi's translation of the Montale essay, "Two Jackals on a
Leash," appeared in *The Second Life of Art: Selected Essays of Eugenio
Montale,* edited and translated by Jonathan Galassi (Ecco Press, New
York, 1982), and is reprinted by permission of the translator and
publisher. Translation © 1982 by Jonathan Galassi.

Publication of this translation has been made possible in part by a grant
to Graywolf Press from the Wheatland Foundation, New York.
Graywolf Press has also received support from the National Endowment
for the Arts, the Minnesota State Arts Board, the McKnight
Foundation, many other corporate, foundation, and individual donors.
Graywolf Press is a member agency of United Arts, Saint Paul.

This book is published by G R A Y W O L F   P R E S S
Post Office Box 75006, Saint Paul, Minnesota 55175. All rights reserved.

I S B N   1-55597-123-7
Library of Congress Number 89-25957
9   8   7   6   5   4   3   2
First Printing, 1990

TABLE OF CONTENTS

INTRODUCTION

by

Dana Gioia

THE MOTETS of Eugenio Montale are a sequence of twenty short poems written between 1934 and 1939. They are not, as some readers have assumed, merely a collection of individual poems linked loosely by a common theme or occasion. Instead they form a unified sequence whose full meaning and power becomes apparent only when they are read together. Individually they are a series of distinguished short poems. Together they constitute one of the great lyric works in modern European poetry.

Collected and published in Montale's second book, *Le occasioni* (*The Occasions,* 1939), this sequence marked a turning point in the poet's career. It showed how under the opprobrious weight of the Fascist regime Montale's imagination turned inward, expressing itself in the deeply personal tone of his mature poetry. The *Motets* were also the first poems he published that could in any conventional sense be called love poems, though the experiences they represent are more complex than what one commonly expects in love poetry. These compressed, intensely private lyrics signaled the direction of his later work and introduced the new personal voice that thirty years later would distinguish his second long sequence of love poems, *Xenia* (1970), written after the death of his wife in 1963.

The *Motets* enjoy a problematic eminence in modern Italian literature. While critics have ranked many of the poems among Montale's finest, they have also represented the sequence as exceptionally obscure. As the preeminent modernist in Italian poetry, Montale's position in his native letters has often been compared to that of T.S. Eliot's in Anglo-American literature. This comparison becomes especially ironic when one observes the tendency among critics to overstate the difficulty in reading both poets' work. Early critics wrote so sharply about the obscurity of Montale's supposedly "hermetic" sequence that in 1950 the poet himself found it necessary to defend his methods in print. His whimsical but pointed essay, "Two Jackals on a Leash," explained the genesis of the sequence and satirized the overly literal approach of most critics. Here Montale insisted on the need for readers to maintain some of the inherent mystery of poetry. "There is a middle road," he wrote, "between understanding nothing and understanding too much, a *juste milieu* which poets instinctively respect more than critics."[1]

Readers for whom poetry is a natural part of their lives will have no difficulty in understanding the *Motets*. They will know that one does not experience poetry – or any art – solely through the intellect but with the whole of one's humanity. They will instinctively read the poems, as Montale has suggested, as "an entirely unmysterious little autobiographical

1. "Two Jackals on a Leash" is reprinted on page 65.

novel." If some sections appear obscure when taken out of context, read together in their narrative sequence their import will become immediately clear. If the poems are often subtle and reticent, if occasionally a detail remains puzzling, the central emotional experience in each section will always come across with force and clarity.

The *Motets* tell a story that no one has trouble understanding: a tale of an impossible love. The poet is irrevocably separated from the woman he loves. From the beginning of the sequence he knows that he has lost her forever, yet he cannot stop himself from needing her. She was the center of his world, and that world is now painfully empty. He thinks back on his own life, remembering how close he came to death in the first World War before he had ever met her, and realizes that even then he had been fated to love her. Now she exists for him only as a memory, and the past is not enough to save him from the hell of his existence.

The poet's life continues aimlessly until the visionary moment in the sixth Motet when he witnesses an odd occurrence: an old man in livery dragging two jackals on a leash through the shopping district of Modena. Suddenly he recognizes it as a sign from her. The world now is transformed from Hell into a mysterious Purgatory that he studies for her traces. Although the poet knows that he is absolutely separated from her in a physical sense, he hopes that through these epiphanies they might still in some inexplicable way enjoy a spiritual union that events cannot alter or destroy. He looks for her continuing presence in signs of an almost sacramental nature in the physical world. Sometimes the miraculous signs appear. More often they do not. The appearance or denial of these epiphanies form the central experience of the *Motets*.

The signs characteristically take the form of some unexpected event or odd detail in an otherwise commonplace situation. These extraordinary occurrences strike a chord of subjective associations in the poet, which makes him feel the presence or absence of his lost lover. When the harsh, mechanical sounds of a train pulling out of a station unexpectedly remind him of the rhythms of a terrifying dance, he wonders if his lover hears the same cruel melody of departure. The sound of a footstep muffled in the snow outside a greenhouse makes him imagine her imminent visitation. The exact associations these signs trigger are subjective since they depend on the private past of the couple, which Montale refuses to reveal. Even the woman's name is never spoken in these poems. Because the personal associations are never explained on a literal level, some critics consider the poems hermetic and obscure. Such objections miss the spirit of the sequence. Poetry can be reticent without being obscure. A special splendor of the *Motets* comes from how intimately they recreate the intense emotion of a doomed romance without ever violating the privacy of the lovers. Each poem dramatizes its particular epiphany in such immediate and apprehensible terms that the private associations behind each moment becomes almost immaterial to the reader's experience.

Most lovers speak a sort of secret language. Their shared private experience gives certain words and images special meanings that no outsider can immediately appreciate. One can sometimes tell that two people are secretly lovers simply by hearing them talk in a group. If the couple laughs at some phrase no one else finds funny or exchange glances at a particular word, a hidden romance is often the cause. No literary critic seems to have noticed the obvious fact that the language of the *Motets* is very much the private language of lovers. A reader who finds a particular section difficult might do well to listen as if he or she were overhearing the intimate conversation of two people who understand every nuance of each other's speech.

Even the literary allusions in the *Motets* belong to this private code. For years critics have puzzled over the number of extremely subtle references to Dante embedded in the poems. Now that the "you" in the sequence has been identified as Irma Brandeis, an American Dante scholar whom Montale met in Florence in 1932, the nature of these allusions seems decidedly less literary than personal. These Dantean echoes, most so quiet that even an educated Italian might not hear them unassisted, are private signals between the lovers. Likewise the intense compression of each section reflects the telegraphic way lovers can converse. The speaker knows exactly what one brief phrase or image will convey to his beloved.

The power of Montale's poetic effects depends on the dramatic concentration of the visionary moments. The *Motets* never tell their story in expansive, novelistic terms. Instead they follow Poe's demands for the intensity, brevity, and purity of lyric poetry. The sequence recreates isolated moments of insight, stripped of their nonessential elements. Everything else in the story is told by implication, and the reader must participate in the reconstruction of the human drama by projecting his or her own private associations to fill in the missing elements of the narrative. The concise and unadorned style also suggests at least one reason why Montale called these poems motets, a term used to describe the short sacred musical compositions for unaccompanied voices in the Roman Catholic Church. His poems also use minimal resources to celebrate mysterious and sacred things.

Montale's emphasis in the *Motets* on compression, concreteness of detail, spare precision of language, and visionary impulse link him to the principles of Imagism that he knew from the work of Pound and Eliot. But in these poems Montale achieved what eluded the English-language Imagists. He went beyond the short lyric to create an extended narrative sequence of intense concentration, visionary organization, and uncompromising modernity. Moreover he accomplished this breakthrough in a manner that was nonetheless widely accessible.

The *Motets* are among the loneliest poems ever written. Here is a world empty of all human contact except the memory of one woman now irretrievably lost. Montale's special achievement is to confront the isolation and futility of human existence and yet find so much cause for celebration. If the world is cruel and indifferent, it also possesses an incomparable magnificence. For Montale's pessimism does not arise from either existential *nausée* or decadent ennui, but from an acceptance of life without any comforting illusions. His vision focuses on the tragic insight ultimately behind all philosophy—the recognition that man's life is meager compared to the inexhaustible and eternal presence of the world. In this sense perhaps Montale seems closer to Sophocles than to Eliot. His vision has more in common with the two ancient Mediterranean philosophies of Stoicism and Epicureanism than with any modern movement. If one wanted to find a comparable sensibility in European poetry, one would turn not to any contemporary but to the other great poet of the

Italian landscape, Lucretius the Epicurean. Like the bleak materialist of ancient Rome, Montale faces the inhumanity of nature, the certainty of death, and still rejoices in the unexpected, precarious gift of life.

Although essentially modernist in form, the *Motets* forge an interesting link with traditional Italian and European poetry. They are an original and unexpected renovation of that great lyric tradition of the Renaissance in which the poet chronicles the history of a romance. As Dante did in *La Vita Nuova,* Montale tells the story of an impossible love, dramatically portraying each painful step the poet must take in learning to accept his fate. In the *Motets,* Montale echoes most of the key themes in the Renaissance cycles. His lover is unapproachable, and, as the poet's passion grows Platonic and ennobling, she gradually becomes more of a guardian angel than a woman of flesh and blood. In the same poems where Montale steered modern Italian poetry away from traditional diction, rhythm, form, and imagery, he also subtly renewed its most conservative sources.

Montale's adaptation of this tradition is particularly revealing. The *Motets* begin where earlier Italian sequences finished – at the end of the romance. He and his lover are separated by a pale as absolute as death. There is no possibility of reconciliation. The *Motets* are addressed to a woman so irrevocably absent that the poet ultimately speaks to himself alone. Although his beloved will never hear, he must speak. This tragic situation underlies all of the *Motets,* giving the poems dignity and force without ever allowing them to become self-pitying or sentimental.

The *Motets* are strikingly original and yet deeply traditional, genuinely modern and still widely accessible. They are love poems about the impossibility of love, celebrations of a world as inhuman as it is beautiful. They mix faith with despair, nightmare with joyful vision. Any description of them sounds paradoxical, but their mysterious scope contributes to their special power. They thoroughly evade any attempt at paraphrase. One cannot do anything but read them – each time with more wonder and surprise.

NOTE ON THE TRANSLATION

My intention in translating the *Motets* has been to recreate them as contemporary poems in English. This objective frequently required me to rethink the phrasing and lineation of the originals so that the new versions would move naturally as English-language poems. The rhythms of Montale's Italian have a tension that holds the conflicting elements of each poem in nervous balance. I therefore resisted the temptation of translating the originals one line at a time since Montale's fluent prosody often loses both its sharpness and poise if rendered too mechanically. Instead I tried to reimagine the total rhythm of each poem and set an English cadence that would integrate the transposed elements tightly into a new whole. As a result the lineation of my translations is sometimes radically different from the original.

I also wanted the translations to work independently in their new language without the need for footnotes. When this objective required adding a word or incorporating a gloss, I did so, always preferring the emotional clarity and narrative integrity of the whole poem in English to the lexicographical fidelity of the individual word. Too often translators of

Montale have upset an entire poem to catch the special flavor of a single unusual phrase. My version of Montale's *Mottetti* is therefore not a paraphrase in Dryden's famous definition but an imitation. My hope is that these translations can be read independently as a successful poetic sequence in English faithful not only to the sense but also the spirit of the Italian.

Dana Gioia

MOTTETTI

The Motets of

Eugenio Montale

Lo sai: debbo riperderti e non posso.
Come un tiro aggiustato mi sommuove
ogni opera, ogni grido e anche lo spiro
salino che straripa
dai moli e fa l'oscura primavera
di Sottoripa.

Paese di ferrame e alberature
a selva nella polvere del vespro.
Un ronzío lungo viene dall'aperto,
strazia com'unghia ai vetri. Cerco il segno
smarrito, il pegno solo ch'ebbi in grazia
da te.
      E l'inferno è certo.

You know this: I must lose you again and cannot.
Every action, every cry strikes me
like a well-aimed shot, even the salt spray
that spills over the harbor walls
and makes spring
dark against the gates of Genoa.

Country of ironwork and ship masts
like a forest in the dust of evening.
A long drone comes from the open spaces
scraping like a nail on a windowpane. I look
for the sign I have lost, the only pledge
I had from you.
                    Now hell is certain.

Molti anni, e uno più duro sopra il lago
straniero su cui ardono i tramonti.
Poi scendesti dai monti a riportarmi
San Giorgio e il Drago.

Imprimerli potessi sul palvese
che s'agita alla frusta del grecale
in cuore ... E per te scendere in un gorgo
di fedeltà, immortale.

Many years, and one of them a little harder
on a foreign lake burning in the sunsets.
Then you came down from the mountains
    to bring me back
Saint George and the Dragon.

If only I could print them on the banner
rising and falling in the brutal wind
of my heart – and descend for you
into a chasm of fidelity, forever.

Brina sui vetri; uniti
sempre e sempre in disparte
gl'infermi; e sopra i tavoli
i lunghi soliloqui sulle carte.

Fu il tuo esilio. Ripenso
anche al mio, alla mattina
quando udii tra gli scogli crepitare
la bomba ballerina.

E durarono a lungo i notturni giuochi
di Bengala: come in una festa.

È scorsa un'ala rude, t'ha sfiorato le mani,
ma invano: la tua carta non è questa.

Frost on the windowpanes; the sick
always with each other yet always
alone; and at the tables long
soliloquies about the cards.

This was your exile. Now I think
of mine again, of the morning when I heard
the bomb they called the "ballerina"
go off between the rocks.

And it lasted a long time – like oriental fireworks
on the evening of a festival.

A hard wing brushed past you, touching your hands,
but to no purpose: this was not your card.

Lontano, ero con te quando tuo padre
entrò nell'ombra e ti lasciò il suo addio.
Che seppi fino allora? Il logorío
di *prima* mi salvò solo per questo:

che t'ignoravo e non dovevo: ai colpi
d'oggi lo so, se di laggiú s'inflette
un'ora e mi riporta Cumerlotti
o Anghébeni – tra scoppi di spolette
e i lamenti e l'accorrer delle squadre.

Far away, still I was with you
when your father
went into darkness and left you his goodbye.
What did I learn
in that moment? That until then
the ravages of the past
had spared me
only for this:

I had not met you yet
and had to. I know this
from the pain of today, and would
even if the hours bent
back on themselves and brought
me once again to Cumerlotti
or Anghébeni, among the exploding
shells, the screams,
the panic of the squadrons.

Addii, fischi nel buio, cenni, tosse
e sportelli abbassati. È l'ora. Forse
gli automi hanno ragione. Come appaiono
dai corridoi, murati!

. . .

– Presti anche tu alla fioca
litania del tuo rapido quest'orrida
e fedele cadenza di carioca? –

The long goodbyes, the whistles in the dark,
the waving, coughing, lowering of windows:
it's time. Maybe
the automatons are right. Staring from the passageways,
they seem buried.

• • •

– Can you hear it too? The harsh
litany of the express, the terrifying,
steady rhythm of a dance?

La speranza di pure rivederti
m'abbandonava;

e mi chiesi se questo che mi chiude
ogni senso di te, schermo d'immagini,
ha i segni della morte o dal passato
è in esso, ma distorto e fatto labile,
un *tuo* barbaglio:

(a Modena, tra i portici,
un servo gallonato trascinava
due sciacalli al guinzaglio).

I had almost lost
hope of ever seeing you again;

and I asked myself if this thing
cutting me off
from every trace of you, this screen
of images,
was the approach of death, or truly
some dazzling
vision of you
out of the past,
bleached, distorted,
fading:

(under the arches at Modena
I saw an old man in a uniform
dragging two jackals on a leash).

Il saliscendi bianco e nero dei
balestrucci dal palo
del telegrafo al mare
non conforta i tuoi crucci su lo scalo
né ti riporta dove piú non sei.

Già profuma il sambuco fitto su
lo sterrato; il piovasco si dilegua.
Se il chiarore è una tregua,
la tua cara minaccia la consuma.

The black and white
flight of swallows rising
and falling in a line
from the telegraph
pole to the sea
does not ease the pain
you feel by the water
nor bring you back
to somewhere
you have left.

The elder tree
already sheds its thick
perfume above the upturned
earth, and the tempest
washes itself away.
If this clear light
signifies a truce,
the sweet threat of you
consumes it.

Ecco il segno; s'innerva
sul muro che s'indora:
un frastaglio di palma
bruciato dai barbagli dell'aurora.

Il passo che proviene
dalla serra sí lieve,
non è felpato dalla neve, è ancora
tua vita, sangue tuo nelle mie vene.

Here is the sign; it trembles
over a wall that is turning
itself to gold:
the fretwork of a palm leaf
burnt by the blinding
dazzle of sunrise.

The sound of steps coming down
so lightly from the greenhouse
is not muffled
by the snow, is still
your life, your blood
in my veins.

Il ramarro, se scocca
sotto la grande fersa
dalle stoppie –

la vela, quando fiotta
e s'inabissa al salto
della rocca –

il cannone di mezzodí
piú fioco del tuo cuore
e il cronometro se
scatta senza rumore –

e poi? Luce di lampo

invano può mutarvi in alcunché
di ricco e strano. Altro era il tuo stampo.

If the green lizard darts
out of the stubble under
the great whip—

the sail flapping with wind
sinks into the nothingness
beyond the rocks—

the cannon at noon sounds
fainter than your heart,
and if the clock
strikes without a sound—

what then? Then it means nothing

that a flash of lightning
can change you into something
rich and strange. You chose another shape.

Perché tardi? Nel pino lo scoiattolo
batte la coda a torcia sulla scorza.
La mezzaluna scende col suo picco
nel sole che la smorza. È giorno fatto.

A un soffio il pigro fumo trasalisce,
si difende nel punto che ti chiude.
Nulla finisce, o tutto, se tu fólgore
lasci la nube.

Why are you waiting? The squirrel in the pine tree
beats its torchlike tail on the bark.
The half-moon sinks with one tip fading
into the sun. The day is finished.

The lazy smoke is startled by a breeze
but gathers itself to cover you.
Nothing will end, or everything, if you,
the flash of lightning, leave the cloud.

L'anima che dispensa
furlana e rigodone ad ogni nuova
stagione della strada, s'alimenta
della chiusa passione, la ritrova
a ogni angolo piú intensa.

La tua voce è quest'anima diffusa.
Su fili, su ali, al vento, a caso, col
favore della musa o d'un ordegno,
ritorna lieta o triste. Parlo d'altro,
ad altri che t'ignora e il suo disegno
è là che insiste *do re la sol sol* . . .

The spirit that scatters ancient
songs and dances into each
new season of the street, feeds on
hidden passion, and finds it
more intense at every corner.

Your voice is this effusive spirit.
On wires, on wings, in the air,
by the accidental blessings of the Muse
or out of some machine, it comes back
happy or sad. I speak of other things
to other people who don't know you,
but your design is always there
insisting, *do re la sol sol* . . .

Ti libero la fronte dai ghiaccioli
che raccogliesti traversando l'alte
nebulose; hai le penne lacerate
dai cicloni, ti desti a soprassalti.

Mezzodí: allunga nel riquadro il nespolo
l'ombra nera, s'ostina in cielo un sole
freddoloso; e l'altre ombre che scantonano
nel vicolo non sanno che sei qui.

I run my hand across your forehead
to wipe away the ice
that formed there as you crossed
the highest clouds. Your wings
have been torn by cyclones.
You wake with a sudden start.

Noon: and the black shadow of the medlar
stretches itself across the square,
a cold sun lingers overhead,
and the other shadows
turning in the alley
don't know that you are here.

La gondola che scivola in un forte
bagliore di catrame e di papaveri,
la subdola canzone che s'alzava
da masse di cordame, l'alte porte
rinchiuse su di te e risa di maschere
che fuggivano a frotte –

una sera tra mille e la mia notte
è piú profonda! S'agita laggiú
uno smorto groviglio che m'avviva
a stratti e mi fa eguale a quell'assorto
pescatore d'anguille dalla riva.

The gondola that glides
forward in the dark
splendor of its polished
tar and poppies, the insinuating
song that rises from beyond
the heaps of rigging, the tall
doors that close behind you,
and the smiles of the masqueraders
who run away in packs –

only one evening out of many,
but my night goes deeper still.
A pale tangle writhing in the water
startles me awake and suddenly
I am joined to the man so intently
fishing for eels on the bank.

Infuria sale o grandine? Fa strage
di campanule, svelle la cedrina.
Un rintocco subacqueo s'avvicina,
quale tu lo destavi, e s'allontana.

La pianola degl'inferi da sé
accelera i registri, sale nelle
sfere del gelo . . . – brilla come te
quando fingevi col tuo trillo d'aria
Lakmé nell'Aria delle Campanelle.

Is it salt or hail raging in the storm,
destroying the bellflowers, toppling
the verbena? That sound again
of underwater tolling, which you
once woke in me, comes closer
and then fades away.

Hell's player piano
is speeding through its rolls,
climbing octaves till it mounts
the icy spheres – glittering there
like you playing Lakmé
as you trilled the *Aria of the Bells*.

Al primo chiaro, quando
subitaneo un rumore
di ferrovia mi parla
di chiusi uomini in corsa
nel traforo del sasso
illuminato a tagli
da cieli ed acque misti;

al primo buio, quando
il bulino che tarla
la scrivanía rafforza
il suo fervore e il passo
del guardiano s'accosta:
al chiaro e al buio, soste ancora umane
se tu a intrecciarle col tuo refe insisti.

At dawn, when suddenly
the noise of a train
speeding through a tunnel
tells me of the men on journeys
trapped in stone,
lit only now and then
by a flash of sky and water:

at dusk when the woodworm
eating slowly through the desk
redoubles its efforts,
and the footsteps of the watchman
come closer:
at dawn and at dusk, even these
moments become human, if you
weave them together with your thread.

Il fiore che ripete
dall'orlo del burrato
non scordarti di me,
non ha tinte piú liete né piú chiare
dello spazio gettato tra me e te.

Un cigolío si sferra, ci discosta,
l'azzurro pervicace non ricompare.
Nell'afa quasi visibile mi riporta all'opposta
tappa, già buia, la funicolare.

The flower on the mountainside,
which keeps repeating its
forget-me-nots from cliff
to cliff, has no colors brighter
or happier than the space
set between us.

A screech of metal is pulling us apart.
The obstinate blue is fading. In a sky
so sultry you can barely
see through it, the funicular
carries me back to the other station
where it's already dark.

XVII

La rana, prima a ritentar la corda
dallo stagno che affossa
giunchi e nubi, stormire dei carrubi
conserti dove spenge le sue fiaccole
un sole senza caldo, tardo ai fiori
ronzío di coleotteri che suggono
ancora linfe, ultimi suoni, avara
vita della campagna. Con un soffio
l'ora s'estingue: un cielo di lavagna
si prepara a un irrompere di scarni
cavalli, alle scintille degli zoccoli.

The frog, first to try its chord again
from the reed-choked, misty pond,
the rustle of the interwoven
carob trees where a cold sun
is snuffing out its own
weak rays, the slow
drone of hornets in the flowers
where there's still a little sap –
the last sounds,
the bare life of the country.
                              One breath
and the hour is extinguished: a sky
the color of slate prepares for the explosion
of death-thin horses, of flaming hooves.

XVIII

Non recidere, forbice, quel volto,
solo nella memoria che si sfolla,
non far del grande suo viso in ascolto
la mia nebbia di sempre.

Un freddo cala ... Duro il colpo svetta.
E l'acacia ferita da sé scrolla
il guscio di cicala
nella prima belletta di Novembre.

Scissors, don't cut away that face,
the last possession of a bankrupt memory,
don't lose her soft, attentive look
in a fog that lasts forever.

The cold descends ... a hard cutting blow,
and the wounded acacia shakes off
the shell of a cicada
into the mud of early November.

La canna che dispiuma
mollemente il suo rosso
flabello a primavera;
la rédola nel fosso, su la nera
correntía sorvolata di libellule;
e il cane trafelato che rincasa
col suo fardello in bocca,

oggi qui non mi tocca riconoscere;
ma là dove il riverbero piú cuoce
e il nuvolo s'abbassa, oltre le sue
pupille ormai remote, solo due
fasci di luce in croce.

     E il tempo passa.

———————————

The reed that sheds its
soft, red crescent
in the spring; the gravel path
above the gully where dragonflies
are hovering on the slow
dark current; the dog,
breathless, coming home
with a bundle in its mouth.

Today there is nothing here
which I can recognize:
but there where the reflection
burns more fiercely and the clouds
descend, there beyond her eyes
which are so distant now, only these two
beams of light that cross.

And time passes.

. . . ma cosí sia. Un suono di cornetta
dialoga con gli sciami del querceto.
Nella valva che il vespero riflette
un vulcano dipinto fuma lieto.

La moneta incassata nella lava
brilla anch'essa sul tavolo e trattiene
pochi fogli. La vita che sembrava
vasta è piú breve del tuo fazzoletto.

... well let it be. Sounds of a cornet
mingle with the bees
swarming in the oak grove. A volcano
painted on a seashell smokes
brightly in the sunset.

Even the old coin set in lava
as a paperweight shines on the table,
holding down a few loose pages.
And this life which seemed so vast
can be spread out on your handkerchief.

TWO JACKALS
ON A LEASH

Eugenio Montale

Translated by Jonathan Galassi

MANY YEARS AGO, a noted poet who has now changed professions, wrote in his head, transcribed onto pieces of paper that he kept balled-up in his jacket pockets, and finally published a series of short poems dedicated, or rather sent by air mail (but only on the wings of the imagination), to a certain Clizia[1] who was living about three thousand miles away. Clizia's real name wasn't Clizia at all; her model can be found in a sonnet of uncertain authorship which Dante, or someone else, sent to Giovanni Quirini;[2] and Mirco's name isn't Mirco either; but my necessary discretion doesn't detract from the import of this note. Let it suffice to identify the typical situation of that poet, and I should say of almost every lyric poet who lives besieged by the absence/presence of a distant woman, in this case a Clizia, who had the name of the woman in the myth who was changed into a sunflower.

Mirco's little poems, which later became a series, an entirely unmysterious little autobiographical novel, were born day by day. Clizia knew nothing about them and may not even have read them until many years later; but every now and then the news of her that reached Mirco provided the impetus for a motet; and thus new epigrams were born and shot off like arrows across the seas, though the interested lady hadn't offered the pretext for them, even involuntarily. Two very different cases, of which I'll give examples. Here is the first:

One day Mirco learned that Clizia's father had died. He felt her loss, and regretted even more deeply the three thousand miles which kept him distant, too distant, from her grief. And it seemed to him that all the anxieties and risks of his life up to that point had converged on a Clizia who was then unknown to him, and on a meeting which would have to wait for many years. Perhaps, he said to himself, the war saved me precisely for this: for without Clizia my life would have had no meaning, no direction. He dredged up his past, saw himself again in certain contested villages in Vallarsa, at Cumerlotti, Anghébeni, under Monte Corvo; he found himself in mortal danger again, but already aided even then, unawares, by Clizia's star, by the umbrella of her sunflower.

That day Mirco sat in a cafe and wrote these lines on the margin of a newspaper, then cast them into the wind, which carried them to their destination:

> *Far away, still I was with you*
> *when your father*
> *went into darkness and left you his goodbye.*
> *What did I learn*
> *in that moment? That until then*
> *the ravages of the past*
> *had spared me*
> *only for this:*

I had not met you yet
and had to. I know this
from the pain of today, and would
even if the hours bent
back on themselves and brought
me once again to Cumerlotti
or Anghébeni, among the exploding
shells, the screams,
the panic of the squadrons.[3]

Second and final example: One summer afternoon Mirco
found himself at Modena walking in the galleries. Anxious as
he was, and still absorbed in his "dominating idea," it aston-
ished him that life could present him with so many distrac-
tions, as if painted or reflected on a screen. It was too gay a
day for a man who wasn't gay. And then an old man in gold-
braided livery appeared to Mirco, dragging two reluctant
champagne-colored puppies on a leash, two little dogs who at
first glance seemed to be neither wolfhounds nor dachshunds
nor Pomeranians. Mirco approached the old man and asked
him, "What kind of dogs are these?" And the old man, dry
and proud, answered, "They're not dogs, they're jackals."
(He spoke like a true, uneducated Southerner, then turned
the corner with his pair.) Clizia loved droll animals. How
amused she would have been to see them! thought Mirco.

And from that day on he never read the name Modena without associating the city with his idea of Clizia and the two jackals. A strange, persistent idea. Could the two beasts have been sent by her, like an emanation? Were they an emblem, an occult signature, a *senhal*? Or were they only an hallucination, the premonitory signs of her fall, her end?

Similar things often happened; there were no more jackals, but other strange products from the grab-bag of life: poodles, monkeys, owls on a trestle, minstrels ... And always, a healing balm entered the heart of the wound. One evening Mirco heard some lines in his head, took a pencil and a tram ticket (the only paper in his pocket) and wrote:

> *I had almost lost*
> *hope of ever seeing you again;*
>
> *and I asked myself if this thing*
> *cutting me off*
> *from every trace of you, this screen*
> *of images,*
> *was the approach of death, or truly*
> *some dazzling*
> *vision of you*
> *out of the past,*
> *bleached, distorted,*
> *fading:*

He stopped, erased the period, and substituted a colon be-
cause he sensed the need for an example that would also be a
conclusion. And he ended:

> *(under the arches at Modena*
> *I saw an old man in a uniform*
> *dragging two jackals on a leash).*[4]

The parentheses were intended to isolate the example and
suggest a different tone of voice, the jolt of an intimate and
distant memory.

When the poems were published with others which were
related and easier to understand, and which ought to have ex-
plained even their two least limpid sisters, great was the baf-
flement of the critics. And the objections of the detractors
were totally out of line with the nature of the case. If the poet
had perhaps abandoned himself too freely to his antecedent,
his "situation," the critics demonstrated a very different, and
more serious, mental torpor.

The first investigations concerned Cumerlotti and
Anghébeni, which were mistaken for two characters essential
to the understanding of the text. Anghébeni, Carneade, who
was he? asked one critic, now a doctor, who we hope brings a
better clinical eye to his new profession. And who, asked
others, was "Cumerlotti's girl"? Were the jackals hers? And
what did Modena have to do with it? Why Modena and not

Parma or Voghera? And the man with the jackals? Was he a servant? A publicist? And the father? How did he die and where and why?

I have touched on one aspect (and only one) of the obscurity or apparent obscurity of certain contemporary art: that which is born of an intense concentration and of a confidence, perhaps excessive, in the material being treated. Faced with this, the critics act like the visitor at an art exhibition who looks at two pictures, a still life of mushrooms, for example, or a landscape with a man walking with an open umbrella, and asks himself: What do these mushrooms cost per pound? Were they picked by the artist or bought at the market? Where is that man going? What's his name? And is that umbrella real silk or synthetic? The obscurity of the classics, not only of Dante and Petrarch but also of Foscolo and Leopardi, has been partly unraveled by the commentary of whole generations of scholars: and I don't doubt that those great writers would be flabbergasted by the exegeses of certain of their interpreters. And the obscurity of certain of the moderns will finally give way too, if there are still critics tomorrow. Then we shall all pass from darkness into light, too much light: the light the so-called aesthetic commentators cast on the mystery of poetry. There is a middle road between understanding nothing and understanding too much, a *juste milieu* which poets instinctively respect more than their critics; but on this side or that of the border there is no safety for either poetry or criticism. There is only a waste-land, too dark or too bright, where two poor jackals cannot live or cannot venture forth without being hunted down, seized, and shut behind the bars of a zoo.

1. Poetic name for the sunflower, after the nymph loved by Apollo, who turned her into a sunflower.
2. Fourteenth-century Venetian writer of ballads and sonnets, and a poetical correspondent of Dante's.
3. *Mottetti* IV translated by Dana Gioia.
4. *Mottetti* VI translated by Dana Gioia.

A NOTE ABOUT EUGENIO MONTALE

Eugenio Montale was born in Genoa in 1896. He was a poet, editor, translator, critic and journalist. His first book of poems, *Ossi di seppia,* was published in 1925 to great acclaim. His sequence of motets was published in 1939 as part of his book *Le occasioni.* While serving as director of the Vieusseux Library in Florence in the late 1930s, Montale was forced to resign because he refused to join the Fascist party. After World War II he became the principal literary critic for the leading Italian newspaper, *Corriere della Sera.* Later in life he returned to writing poetry and was awarded the Nobel Prize for Literature in 1975. He died in Milan on September 12, 1981.

Dana Gioia was born in Los Angeles in 1950. He received B.A. and M.B.A. degrees from Stanford University as well as an M.A. in Comparative Literature from Harvard University. His poems have appeared in many magazines including the *New Yorker, Paris Review, Poetry,* and *Hudson Review,* and were collected in his book *Daily Horoscope* (Graywolf Press, 1986). With William Jay Smith, he edited *Poems from Italy* (New Rivers Press, 1986). Mr. Gioia is an executive with a major American corporation and lives outside New York City with his wife and son.

A NOTE ON THE BOOK

This book was designed by Tree Swenson.

The Imprint type was designed for the periodical of the same name, instigated by Gerald Meynell, J.H. Mason, Ernest Jackson, and Edward Johnston. The type was set by The Typeworks, Vancouver, B.C.

The book was manufactured by Arcata Graphics.